Earth's Place in Space

by Elizabeth Alexander

PEARSON

Scott
Foresman

Editorial Offices: Glenview, Illinois • Parsippany, New Jersey • New York, New York
Sales Offices: Needham, Massachusetts • Duluth, Georgia • Glenview, Illinois
Coppell, Texas • Ontario, California • Mesa, Arizona

SBN: 0-328-13607-7

4 5 6 7 8 9 10 V0G1 14 13 12 11 10 09 08 07 06

CONTENTS

Chapter 1 Studying Space

For thousands of years, people have looked at the sky in wonder. They have carefully observed the movement of the moon, the stars, and other heavenly bodies. Ancient people did not have battery-powered clocks or pocket calendars. They used the sun to tell the time of day. They used the moon to tell the time of the month and the coming and going of a year. Nearly every culture on Earth had a way to record time using the sky.

Stonehenge in England is thought to have been a giant calendar used to predict the seasons.

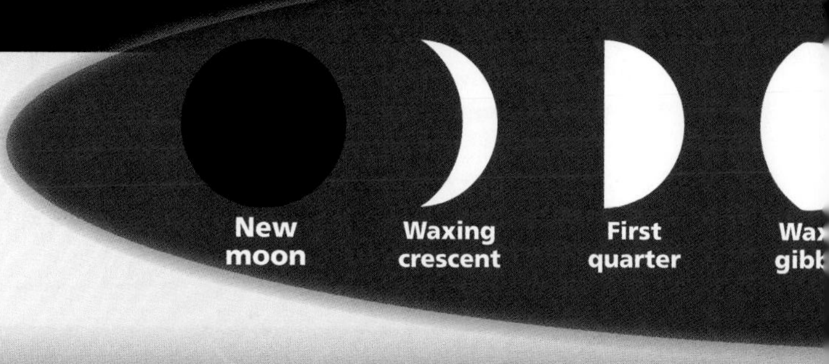

New
moon

Waxing
crescent

First
quarter

Wax
gibb

For example, Native Americans noted that each month the moon waxes and wanes (grows and shrinks). It changes shape in a cycle that contains several stages. The different shapes are known as phases of the moon. Eight phases make one cycle.

Native Americans gave particular moon cycles names such as Laying Geese and Coming Caribou. They chose these names by observing what was happening in nature at the same time. Some northern and eastern tribes called the moon the Snow Moon in February because that is generally when the most snow fell. The Hunter's Moon appeared in October, when deer for hunting were plentiful.

The ancient Egyptians based their entire calendar on the rising of a particular star they called *Sirius*. The day that it rose with the sun was the first day of the year. Like ours, their year lasted 365 days. However, the Egyptians did not account for the extra quarter day as we do. Every four years, we add a day to our year to make up for the extra quarter day. A year with this extra day is called a leap year.

Every four years, Sirius rose one day earlier, and their year started one day sooner. This cycle would right itself every 1,460 years, when Sirius would rise with the sun again.

The Phases of the Moon

Full moon — Waning gibbous — Last quarter — Waning crescent — New moon

Early Astronomy

Ancient people saw the shapes of animals and objects in groups of stars called constellations. Perhaps you know the constellation Leo. If you draw a line from one star to another in Leo, you can see the rough shape of a lion.

Astronomer, mathematician, and geographer Ptolemy lived in Egypt from about A.D. 100 to A.D. 170. He noticed that as the seasons change, the stars and planets change position in the sky. His observations led him to believe that constellations move around Earth, while Earth stays still. Ptolemy's conclusion made sense based on what he saw. Even before his time, other ideas had emerged about the positions of the planets and stars. As better tools were invented, most of these ideas were proven wrong.

Leo is one of the many constellations in the night sky.

The Sun at the Center

Aristarchus (310–230 B.C.) was an early astronomer. An astronomer is a scientist who studies space and the position of the planets and stars. He proposed that the sun was at the center of the universe. He believed that Earth moved around the Sun. Aristarchus was partially right. The sun is not the center of the universe, but Earth does move around the sun. Very few people believed his idea.

About 1,800 years passed. A Polish **astronomer** named Copernicus restated what Aristarchus had said. In 1543 Copernicus said that Earth and other planets move around the sun. Even then, many people did not want to believe it.

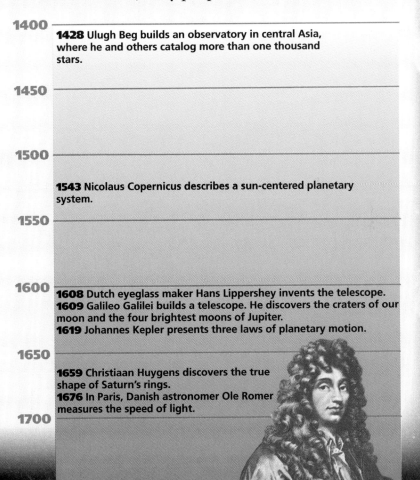

1400

1428 Ulugh Beg builds an observatory in central Asia, where he and others catalog more than one thousand stars.

1450

1500

1543 Nicolaus Copernicus describes a sun-centered planetary system.

1550

1600

1608 Dutch eyeglass maker Hans Lippershey invents the telescope.
1609 Galileo Galilei builds a telescope. He discovers the craters of our moon and the four brightest moons of Jupiter.
1619 Johannes Kepler presents three laws of planetary motion.

1650

1659 Christiaan Huygens discovers the true shape of Saturn's rings.
1676 In Paris, Danish astronomer Ole Romer measures the speed of light.

1700

Christiaan Huygens

Johannes Kepler (left) explains his theory concerning planetary motion to his sponsor, Emperor Rudolf II (right).

Astronomers' Observations

The time line on page 7 shows some important achievements in the early history of astronomy. Many astronomers built on the discoveries of those who came before them.

For example, find Johannes Kepler on the time line. Kepler lived from 1571 to 1630, in what is now Germany. He studied with an astronomer named Tycho Brahe. By carefully studying his teacher's observations, Kepler discovered that the planets do not orbit the sun in perfectly round circles, but in elongated circles called ellipses.

Galileo Galilei improved upon magnification tools for his work. In December of 1609 Galileo Galilei built a telescope that magnified objects fifteen to twenty times. Using this telescope, he discovered mountains and craters on the moon.

Chapter 2 The Sun, Planets, Moons, and More

We now know a lot about the objects that float through space. Our solar system is made up of nine planets—Mercury, Venus, Earth, Mars, Jupiter, Saturn, Uranus, Neptune, and Pluto. Mercury is the closest to the sun, and Pluto is the farthest away.

There are also at least sixty known moons that orbit seven of the planets. Some planets, like Earth, have only one moon. Others, like Jupiter, have several moons. Comets, asteroids, gases, and dust can also be found in the solar system.

Everything in our solar system orbits—revolves around— the sun, which sits at the center of the solar system. Our solar system is part of a larger **galaxy** called the Milky Way, which in turn is one of billions of galaxies in the universe.

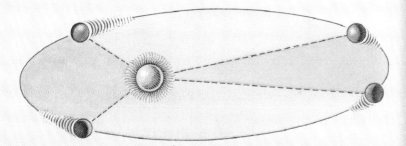

An illustration of Kepler's second law of planetary motion shows a planet orbiting the sun in an elliptical orbit.

Saturn, Uranus, and Neptune have rings. Of those, Saturn's are the best known.

The Planets

The word *planet* comes from the ancient Greek word *planasthai*. The Greek word means "to wander." Ancient people who studied the sky observed five wandering objects that we call Mercury, Venus, Mars, Jupiter, and Saturn. These are the planets that people can see using only their eyes. You don't need a telescope to see them.

Early astronomers noticed that the planets wandered through the constellations. However, when they looked at the stars, they seemed to stay in the same place in relation to each other.

After all nine planets had been discovered, astronomers classified them into three groups. The inner planets—Mercury, Venus, Earth, and Mars—are closest to the sun. They are similar in their composition as each has a metal core.

The outer planets—Jupiter, Saturn, Uranus, and Neptune—are nicknamed the "gas giants." They don't have a solid crust, and most of their volume is made up of gas. However, it is believed that their cores are solid.

Pluto, a ball of ice and rock, is in a group of its own. However, some scientists classify it as an outer planet. It is the smallest planet in our solar system, smaller than some moons. In recent years, some scientists have even questioned whether Pluto is a planet at all because of its small size.

Gravity

The force that holds the planets in orbit around the sun is the same force that holds you on Earth and determines how much you weigh. That force is gravity, which pulls any two objects toward each other.

The planets orbit the sun because the sun's gravity pulls them toward it. The moon orbits Earth because Earth's gravity pulls on the moon.

The strength of gravity between two objects depends partly on their mass. The sun has a much greater mass than the planets. So, the planets orbit the sun, not the other way around. Earth, which has a greater mass than the moon, does not orbit its **satellite.** Instead, the moon orbits Earth.

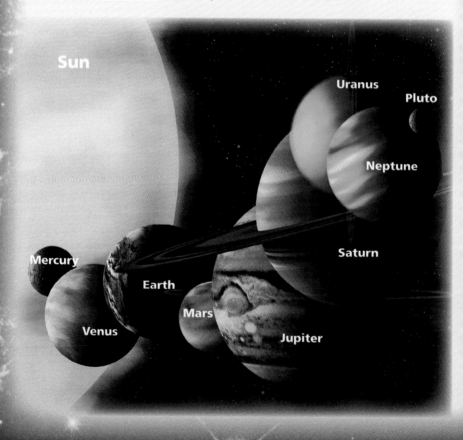

Sun

Uranus

Pluto

Neptune

Saturn

Mercury

Earth

Mars

Venus

Jupiter

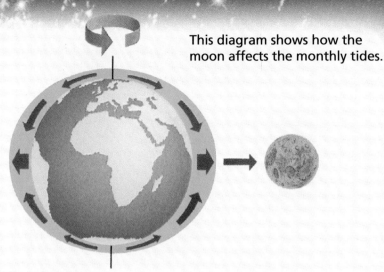

This diagram shows how the moon affects the monthly tides.

The Tides

The strength of gravity between two objects also depends on the distance between them. This helps explain why we have low ocean tides and high ocean tides.

As the moon orbits Earth, the moon's gravity pulls on the ocean waters on the surface of the planet. The pull is stronger on the side of Earth that is closest to the moon. So high tides occur on the side of Earth that the moon is facing.

On the opposite side of Earth, the sun is having the same effect. This creates high tide on this side of Earth as well. Low tides occur in the regions in between the gravitational effects of the moon and the sun.

The "family" of planets that orbit the sun

A supermassive star can be seen from within the Pistol nebula.

Chapter 3 How the Solar System Formed

There have been many theories concerning how the solar system formed. Because it happened so long ago, it is hard to find clues that might give scientists a definite answer.

Even today, scientists don't always agree. With every new piece of information gathered from space probes and missions into the solar system, theories about the formation of the sun and planets change.

However, most scientists agree that the solar system formed about 4 to 5 billion years ago. Some scientists think that it all began in deep space, with a giant cloud of gas and dust.

A Collapsing Cloud

Something happened to disturb the cloud, though scientists are not sure what. Perhaps a star exploded. (Large stars can die in huge explosions.)

The explosion produced shock waves that **collided** with the cloud of gas and dust. The shock waves caused the **particles** in the cloud to pack together.

Gravity may have played a role as well. Remember, gravity is a force that pulls any two objects together. It pulled together the gas and dust. The gravity between these objects was so strong that the cloud began to **collapse,** and spin around.

This **compact** cloud spun faster and faster as it collapsed more and more. It developed a core that was hot and dense. A disk of gas and dust—hot at the center but cool at the edges—surrounded the core, creating a nebula.

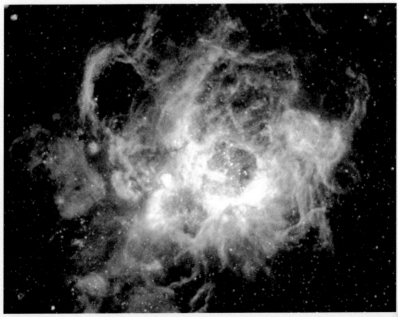

NGC 604 is the largest known nebula. Our own solar system may have started out as a nebula.

Tens of thousands of years went by. The disk of gas and dust got very thin. It was so thin that it flattened out. Particles of dust inside the disk began to collide, stick together, and form clumps.

The two main parts of the cloud, its core and disk, became the bodies in our solar system. The core became the sun. The clumps that formed from the disk became the planets, moons, and asteroids.

Inner and Outer Planets

Turn back to page 11 and reread the section on the inner and outer planets. Now that you have learned how the solar system formed, you can understand something more about these two groups.

The inner part of the collapsing cloud that became the solar system was warmer than the outer part. The inner planets were formed near the part of the cloud that became the sun. It was so hot there that the elements **condensed.** They changed from a gas into a liquid or solid. So, the cores and outer layers of the inner planets—Mercury, Venus, Earth, and Mars—are made up of rock and metal.

The gas giants came from the cloud's outer regions, where it was cooler. It was so cool in the outer regions that ices made of water and a compound called methane condensed. So, the gas giants—Jupiter, Saturn, Uranus, and Neptune—are primarily made up of gas. However scientists believe that they may have solid cores.

The Hubble Space Telescope transmitted many images of the Whirlpool Galaxy back to Earth. This image shows what this spiral galaxy looks like.

A white dwarf star

The End of the Solar System

Stars change over time. At about 5 billion years old, our sun is a middle-aged star. Like other stars, our sun will die one day.

Some astronomers predict that in 5 billion years the sun will become much larger. It will become a kind of star called a red giant. At this stage in the sun's life, most of the inner planets will be destroyed.

Some scientists believe that after another 1 billion years, the sun will be an old star that will no longer make heat and light. It will shrink to the size of a small planet and become a white dwarf. This is the last stage in the life cycle of a star.

Chapter 4 The Milky Way

If you live in or visit the countryside, look at the sky on a clear night. You may see part of our galaxy, the Milky Way. The Milky Way is made up of about 200 billion stars.

Astronomers tell us that there are billions of galaxies in the universe. So, hundreds of billions of stars are illuminating, or lighting up, outer space. However, most of them are so far away that we cannot see them clearly.

Stars move in orbit around the center of a galaxy, just as planets in our solar system move in orbit around the sun. The whole solar system, including Earth, moves with the sun around the center of the Milky Way. It takes Earth 365 days to orbit the sun. It takes the sun about 250 million years to orbit the galaxy.

The Milky Way was named for the way it looks from Earth. People have long observed that the part of the galaxy that we can see looks like a giant milk spill in the sky. The ancient Romans called it Via Lactea. *Via* means "road" or "way." *Lactea* means "milk."

This is an image of what astronomers think the Milky Way looks like from its edge.

The Milky Way is a spiral galaxy.

We now call the entire galaxy the Milky Way. It looks like a pinwheel with a thick bright center—called the bulge—and flat edges. The picture on this page shows what the Milky Way may look like from above. Scientists have not been able to send a space probe outside the galaxy in order to get an accurate picture. Instead, they base their hypotheses on what other galaxies look like. This "outside view" reveals the true shape of our galaxy. It is a spiral.

Not all stars are confined to the flat part of the galaxy. There are some older stars that can be found above and below the spiraling arms of the Milky Way. They make up what is called the halo of the galaxy.

Our sun lies on the inner edge of the galaxy in a spiral arm. The sun's position in the galaxy is similar to the outer planets' position in the solar system. The sun is far from the center of the Milky Way. That's why it takes millions of years for the sun to orbit the galactic center just one time.

Astronomers classify galaxies based on their shapes. There are four types of galaxies: spiral, barred spiral, elliptical, and irregular. A spiral galaxy looks like a sea star (starfish) or pinwheel with a bulge at the center.

The newer stars in a spiral galaxy are in the arms. The older stars are at the center. Since the sun can be found in one of the spiral arms, scientists can conclude that it is one of the younger stars in the Milky Way.

Galaxy M87, a giant elliptical galaxy 50 million light years away

An elliptical galaxy is made up mostly of older stars. The shape of elliptical galaxies varies a bit. Some are spherical, like planets. Others look more like footballs.

Some of the largest and smallest galaxies are elliptical. The largest elliptical galaxies are giants. They contain one trillion or more stars. The smallest elliptical galaxies are known as dwarfs. Nine elliptical dwarfs are satellites of the Milky Way.

Irregular galaxies are the least common of the four types. As you can tell by their name, their shape is irregular; that is, they cannot be classified as spiral or elliptical in shape.

One spiral galaxy looks much like another spiral galaxy. Elliptical galaxies also look similar to each other. However, each irregular galaxy has a different shape.

Two irregular galaxies orbit the Milky Way. These galaxies are known as the Magellanic Clouds. They are named after the explorer Ferdinand Magellan. His crew spotted them in the sky on their first trip around the world. They are so close to our galaxy and shine so brightly that you can see them without the aid of a telescope.

They are classified as Large Magellanic Cloud and Small Magellanic Cloud. But don't go looking for them if you live in North America. You must be south of the equator to observe them. The center of the Milky Way is also visible from the Southern Hemisphere, in the constellation Sagittarius.

The next time you are outside on a clear night, look up at the sky. See how many of these stars, planets, and galaxies you can spot!

This image from the Hubble Space Telescope includes many spiral galaxies.

Glossary

astronomer *n.* an expert in astronomy, the science that deals with the sun, moon, planets, stars, etc.

collapse *v.* to shrink together suddenly; to cave in.

collided *v.* hit or struck violently together; crashed.

compact *adj.* firmly packed together, closely joined.

condensed *v.* made or became denser or more compact.

galaxy *n.* a group of billions of stars forming one system.

particles *n.* very tiny bits of matter.

satellite *n.* an object that revolves around a planet; it can be either astronomical or human-made.